Making compost

Gardening **organically**

One of the great joys of gardening is to experience the variety of life that a healthy garden contains. A garden managed using organic methods will have far more interest in it than a garden where insecticides and chemicals are used. An organic garden is a more balanced environment, where 'good' creatures such as ladybirds and beetles keep the 'bad' pests and diseases under control.

Organically grown plants also tend to be healthier and stronger than plants that rely on large doses of artificial fertiliser. In healthy soil they grow strong roots and can better withstand attack by pests and diseases. Soil can be kept in top condition by recycling garden waste to make nutritious compost. Growing the right combination of plants in the right place at the right time – by rotating where you plant your veg for example, or choosing shrubs to suit the growing conditions that your garden can offer – can deliver impressive disease-free results.

These are the basic principles of organic growing – use the natural resources you already have to create a balanced and vibrant garden. It's sustainable, cheaper than buying chemicals, easier than you think and great fun. Enjoy your organic gardening.

Compost is a miracle of nature – you put in rubbish and you get out (all being well) some lovely dark and crumbly fertiliser – which when added to your garden improves the soil and helps keep plants healthy.

This book gives you tried and tested, practical advice to help you recycle garden and kitchen waste at home – whatever the size of your garden. It explains how you can make garden compost, leafmould and mulches to feed your garden and keep it healthy – at little or no cost.

Recycling these materials is the foundation for sustainable organic gardening – it eliminates the need to use artificial fertilisers and plays a big part in creating stronger, more pest-resistant plants. It also cuts the environmental pollution that burning or dumping causes. Everyone wins when you compost.

Contents

6

1

Making compost

What is compost and why make it?

Garden compost looks just like rich dark soil – but it really is 'magic' stuff as far as the garden is concerned. It lightens heavy, sticky, clay soils, helps light, sandy soils to hold water and generally keeps ordinary soils in good condition. It achieves this magic by encouraging soil life - microbes, worms and other tiny creatures that live in the soil. This not only improves the nutritional quality of the soil but it improves its consistency as well.

Compost provides plant foods in a natural, balanced form. It is excellent food for all the microbes, worms and other creatures that live in the soil. As they feed on it, the compost is mixed with the soil to improve its structure, and the goodness it contains is gradually made available to plants.

Another benefit of making compost is that it can help your plants resist pests and diseases. Plants grown on composted soils often do better than those fed with artificial fertilisers. Compost can also help to keep pests and diseases living in the soil in check.

All in all, not bad for a product that started life as a heap of weeds, vegetable scraps and other so-called rubbish!

Choosing a method of composting

In nature, plants and animals that die decay and disappear into the earth. When making compost in the garden you are just harnessing the natural decay process to obtain the end product you want, in the timescale that suits you.

There are different methods that you can use to recycle kitchen and garden waste depending on the type and volume of waste available (which may vary at different times of year) and the time and energy you want to give to the process.

- Kitchen and garden waste available now and again, often in quite small quantities – cool heap page 41
- Mixed garden waste available in large quantities over a short period of time – hot heap page 43
- Kitchen waste only – worm composting
- Woody and evergreen prunings – dealing with woody waste page 30
- Autumn leaves in quantity – leafmould heap page 33

  If you are not sure which method is for you, start with the cool heap on page 41.

Creatures in the compost heap

The amazing thing about the composting process is that it is all done for you – by billions and billions of tiny creatures, most of them microscopic. There are more microbes in a teaspoon of compost than there are people on the planet, and they appear in the heap naturally, as if by magic.

Larger creatures, such as woodlice, beetles and worms also get involved.

Some creatures may simply use a compost heap for warmth or shelter.

So don't get alarmed if you open the lid of your compost bin and it seems to be heaving with wildlife – they are only doing their job.

Creatures you might find in a compost heap:
Fungi and bacteria
Earwigs
Ground beetles
Money spiders
Compost worms
Grass-snake eggs
Millipedes
Centipedes
Slugs and snails
Ants
Field mice
Toads
Garden spiders
Harvestmen
Beetles
Larvae
Voles
Woodlice

10 good reasons to make compost

- Helps your garden and the environment
- Is the most environmentally effective method of dealing with kitchen and garden waste
- Naturally nourishes the soil, and hence the plants
  - a key principle of organic gardening
- Cuts trips to the tip and waste going to landfill
- It is satisfying to making a valuable product out of scrap
- Saves money you would have spent on fertiliser
- Grows healthy plants with naturally recycles nutrients
- Cuts the need for watering
- Makes heavy soils easier to work
- Harnesses a natural process to release nutrients back into the soil

2

Getting started

Compost **bins**

You can make compost simply by making a heap of suitable materials and covering it with a sheet of plastic. Most people prefer to make compost in some form of container – a compost bin – with a lid. A compost bin can be home-made or purchased (by mail order or from garden centres). Many local authorities now offer discounted compost bins to householders as a way of encouraging home composting and cutting down on waste going to landfill.

Why use a compost bin?

- It looks a lot neater than a heap

- It stops the composting materials from drying out

- It stops weed seeds blowing onto the compost

- It helps prevent weeds growing in the compost

- It keeps the rain out

Many local authorities offer discounted compost bins to householders – check with yours to see what schemes are available.

15

A compost bin may be anything from a makeshift home-made construction to a purpose-made bin. There are plenty on the market these days, generally made from recycled plastic (green, grey or black) or wood. You can make your own out of wood, breeze blocks, old pallets or wire mesh lined with cardboard for example.

The quality of the compost produced is determined much more by how you use the container, than by the container itself. As long as a compost bin meets certain basic criteria any container will do.

Large quantities of autumn leaves can be recycled on their own to make leafmould (see page 33). A proper compost bin is not required for making leafmould.

If you are buying a compost bin, check that it meets the criteria listed on page 18 before you buy.

Quantities of autumn leaves can be recycled on their own to make leafmould.

A compost bin may be anything from a makeshift home-made construction to a factory-made bin. Examples include a simple wire mesh bin (below left), a home-made New Zealand box (top) and one of many types of purpose-made compost bin (below right).

Features of a good compost bin

- **Lid that is easy to remove and replace**

- **A lid that won't blow off**

- **Decent sized top opening**

- **Sturdy construction**

- **Solid, or almost solid, sides**

- **Open at the bottom (or very well drained base)**

- **Volume 300–750 litres or 90–100cm cube**

Where to put the bin?

You can start composting with a single bin. When it is full, you just lift the bin off the heap (or empty the box if you are using a static container) and start using it again. With two bins, or one double one, you can have one in use while the other is maturing.

Site the bin

- On soil or grass, if possible - if you can only set it on a hard surface put a thick layer of newspaper in the bottom of the bin to soak up liquid that will drain off

- Where access is easy, with a wheelbarrow if you use one

- With working space around it

- In a permanent or temporary location

Some bins require support from posts set in the ground – so they need a permanent site. Bins that are easy to move can be dotted around the garden and moved as required. The soil under a compost heap can be very fertile and is a good spot to grow a courgette or a tomato for example, if a bin is moved.

Kitchen **caddies**

Keep a container handy in the kitchen to hold fruit and veg scraps until you can take them to the compost heap. You can buy a purpose made 'caddy' with a lid and a handle. Some local authority home composting schemes supply them with the compost bin. A recycled plastic food tub will do the job too.

It is advisable to have a container that will not hold more than a few days worth of scraps, so you empty it frequently. Toss in used kitchen paper, paper bags, egg cartons and similar items to soak up any liquid. They can be added to the compost heap too.

action stations

1 **Buy or make** a compost bin that suits your garden.

2 **Ask your local authority** if they supply discounted bins.

3 **Site the bin on bare soil,** where it's easy to get to.

4 **Line** a home-made wire mesh or pallet bin with cardboard.

Raw materials for making compost

What can I compost?

Compost is made from items that were living recently. These materials are broken down by a host of microbes and other tiny creatures. Tin cans, bottles and other items not of living origin will not compost.

> Composting materials rot at different rates, depending on how tough they are. They can be divided, roughly, into:
>
> **'Greens'**
>
> **'Browns'**
>
> **'Green & browns'**

To make good compost you need a mixture of 'greens' and 'browns' in the compost heap. The proportions do not have to be exact, and you will learn the right balance by experience.

Air and water are essential for the creatures that are doing the composting. Air is trapped in the heap as you build it. Water is present in sappy young plant growth, but more may need to be added to dry materials.

The final ingredients - the myriad creatures that do the work - arrive of their own accord.

Most materials for composting will be a mixture of 'green' and 'brown'. The proportion will vary depending on the age of the material. A mixture of these materials helps make good compost – (see pages 26-27 for more detail).

'Greens' (activators) get the composting process started. They are rich in easily accessible nitrogen, which the bugs that do the decomposing need to start work. 'Greens' include: grass mowings, young weeds, young plant material, nettles and comfrey leaves.

'Greens'

Greens are tender young plant materials that are quick to rot. Greens are low in fibre, so on their own they turn to sludge rather than compost. If there are too many ' greens' in a compost heap it will tend to be wet and to smell unpleasant.

'Greens' are also classed as 'activators' as they get the composting process started. They are rich in easily accessible nitrogen, which the bugs that do the decomposing need to start work.

- Grass mowings
- Young plant material
- Comfrey leaves
- Young weeds
- Nettles

Poultry manures and nitrogen-rich liquids, such as urine (diluted 1 in 4 with water) and comfrey or nettle tea - also work as activators.

You can buy various types of compost activator including herbal preparations and mixtures of composting microbes. Some people find these useful. There is no point in buying the type of activator that is simply a nitrogen fertiliser, as one of the natural activators listed above will do the job just as well.

'Green & browns'

Most materials for composting will be a mixture of 'green' and 'brown'. The proportion of 'green' to 'brown' will vary depending on the age of the material. A mixture of these materials would make good compost:

Annual weeds	Poisonous plants
Green leaves	Woollen jumpers
Vegetable trimmings	Feathers
Vegetable peelings	Hay
Flowers	Hair
Bedding plants	Potato tops
Privet hedge clippings	Potato peel
Young, soft hedge clippings	Strawy horse and cattle manures
Soft prunings	Chicken manure with straw
Perennial weeds (see also p35)	Old/weathered straw
Vegetarian pet bedding	Fruit peel, including citrus
Carrot tops	Coffee grounds
Rhubarb leaves	Tea leaves and bags

Other items

Eggshells are safe to add to a compost heap. Their remains can often be seen in mature compost, but this is not a problem. Wood ash can also be added to a compost heap; it is a good source of minerals.

For items not to compost, see page 37.

Balancing 'browns'

A common problem with garden compost is too high a proportion of 'greens', such as grass mowings, in the mix. This makes the compost wet and smelly. Some of the tougher items on the previous page can help to redress the balance - but you may also need to add some 'browns'. These are tough, fibrous items that, on their own, would be very slow to decay. They are best shredded or chopped before being added to a heap, and watered if dry. In large quantities they are generally best recycled separately.

Autumn leaves – see page 33 for dealing with large quantities
Tough hedge clippings and evergreen prunings – see page 30 for dealing with large quantities
Low grade paper and cardboard – see following page 29 for more information
Straw

Composting **paper products**

Paper and cardboard can be useful materials to add to a compost heap. They soak up excess liquid, help to stop the heap becoming too acid, and provide fibre. This makes them ideal ingredients where there is a lot of kitchen waste or grass mowings to recycle.

Cardboard boxes	*Cereal boxes*	*Loo roll middles*
Paper egg boxes	*Used kitchen paper*	*Paper towels and tissues*
Paper bags	*Corrugated cardboard*	*Junk mail*

Whatever the paper, it should be scrumpled up into balls before being added to the compost heap. This introduces air in the mixture so the microbes can keep working. **Never put in flat sheets of paper.**

Composting is not the best method of recycling large quantities of paper; it is better recycled to make more paper.

Most materials for composting will be a mixture of 'green' and 'brown' with the proportion of 'green' to 'brown' varying depending on the age of the material. A mixture of these materials would make good compost.

Dealing with **woody materials**

Woody and evergreen prunings are slow to decay. They often come in large quantities (after cutting a hedge for example) that would overwhelm a conventional compost heap.

If such material can be shredded, it can be recycled to make a useful mulching material. An alternative, if you have the space, is to heap it up in an out-of-the-way corner and leave it to rot for a few years. In the meantime it will make a great habitat for all sorts of creatures.

Where neither of the above is an option, take woody and evergreen material to your local civic amenity site for composting, or put it in your green bin if you have a service that collects garden waste.

Freshly shredded prunings can be used for a mulch on pathways. Otherwise they should be composted before use.

Woody and evergreen materials are slow to decay and would overwhelm most compost heaps. Such material can be shredded and used to make mulch.

Shredded prunings compost heap

- Put the prunings through a shredder

- Fill a compost bin with the shreddings. Water the material as you fill the container. Add alternate layers of grass mowings, or use a nitrogen-rich liquid to water the prunings.

- Cover the heap.

- Within a few days the heap may heat up.

- Leave to compost for 3 months or more. By this time the contents of the heap will **not** have turned into compost, but it should be a dark brown colour. It could be used at this stage as a light-excluding mulch to keep weeds down on shrubberies and other established plantings.

Shredding **tips**

- Buy or hire a shredder – the biggest you can afford

- Some local authorities offer a free shredding service

- Always wear protective goggles and gloves

- Shred outdoors or in a well ventilated area

- Wear a dust mask and work in a well ventilated area when shredding poisonous plants such as laurel

Fallen autumn leaves are very slow to decay. However, they do make a useful balancing 'brown' in a compost heap.

Recycling **autumn leaves**

Fallen autumn leaves are very slow to decay. However, they do make a useful balancing 'brown' in a compost heap. Recycle large quantities separately to make what is known as **leafmould**. Leafmould is a brilliant soil conditioner, mulch and potting compost ingredient. It can be used anywhere in the garden – on veg, fruit, ornamentals and grass - at any time of year.

Making **leafmould**

Collect up fallen autumn leaves. All types, other than evergreens can be used. This is best done after rain, otherwise they must be watered as dry leaves take much longer to decay.

Pack the leaves into a plastic sack, or a leafmould container.

Tie sacks loosely at the top and punch a few holes in the sides. Stack them up in an out of the way spot.

After a year the leafmould can be used as a mulch. After 18-24 months it should be decayed enough to dig in to the soil.

Leafmould tip

Run a mower over leaves that have fallen on a lawn. This shreds them, mixes in grass mowings and collects them up all in one go. This will decay much more quickly than whole leaves.

Leafmould containers

A leafmould bin simply has to stop the leaves blowing away. Use chicken wire or clematis netting to make a square or cylindrical container.

A simple leafmould container can be made from chicken wire or clematis netting.

Recycling **perennial weeds**

Perennial weeds such as dandelions and bindweed can be difficult to eradicate because they regenerate from roots, bulbils or other parts that can survive disturbance. Often a new plant can grow from just a small piece of root or stem. Perennial weeds such as couch grass, dandelions and docks are rich in minerals however, so it is a waste not to recycle them where you can.

Fortunately there are ways of doing this without spreading the weed further. There are a few particularly persistent weeds, such as oxalis, celandine and japanese knotweed that it is best not to recycle at home if you are trying to eradicate them from your garden.

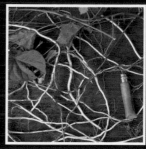

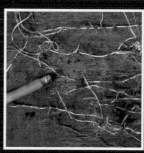

Some perennial weeds are rich in minerals. Nettle (top), bindweed (middle) and couch (bottom) can be composted in a separate 'weed heap' to recycle the goodness they contain.

Smaller quantities of perennial weeds can be mixed with 'green' activators such as lawn mowings and composted in a plastic bag.

The **weed heap**

For larger quantities of perennial weeds.
Pile the weeds up into a heap on their own to compost. Water, and balance the 'green'/'brown' mix, as necessary. Cover the heap with a sheet of black plastic, weighted down around the edges. Use the compost when all signs of life have gone in a year or two.

The black **plastic bag trick**

For smaller quantities of perennial weeds.
Put smaller quantities of perennial weeds into a sturdy plastic sack. The bags that potting compost come in are useful here. Mix in some grass mowings or other 'green' activator (see page 26 if the weeds are mostly roots). Tie the top of the bag, then leave it in an out of the way spot (in the sun if possible) until the contents have rotted to a black sludge. Add the sludge to a compost heap after 6-12 months, when no signs of life are visible.

If neither option suits, take the weeds to a recycling site for composting.

Do not compost the following items!

Not everything that would compost is suitable for adding to a domestic compost heap. The following are best avoided:

Meat and fish scraps   *Bones*

Cooked food leftovers   *Used dog or cat litter*

Dog poo   *Thorny prunings*

Disposable nappies   *Some diseased plants*
                            (see page 58 Q and A)

The following items are not of living origin, and will not compost:

Crisp packets   *Plastic bags*

Tins and cans   *Drinks cartons with plastic liners*

Foam packaging   *Coal ash*

Stones   *Plastic bottles*

Where appropriate, take these items to a recycling centre.

action stations

1 **Compost as much as you can.** The more you put on a heap the better the compost.

2 **Collect low grade paper and cardboard** to balance soggy items on the compost heap.

3 **Never burn autumn leaves.** Collect them to make leafmould.

4 **Recycle perennial weeds separately.**

Starting compost production

Bindweed, nettle and couch grass (above) can be composted into a separate 'weed heap'. Collect and cover them in plastic and leave until well rotted – decomposition may take a year or two.

Tips for successful composting

- Use a mixture of materials to get a balance between 'greens' and 'browns'

- Chop or shred bulky items

- Water dry ingredients or mix with moister items

- Use a bin or a covered heap

- Don't add too many grass mowings

- Use a bin with no base to allow good drainage

- Mix types of ingredients so that air is trapped in the heap

- Choose a method that suits your garden and your lifestyle

Slow, cool composting

A slow, cool heap is an effective method of composting that everyone can use – making compost in around 6-12 months.

Simply fill a compost bin over a period of weeks or months, as materials become available, following the tips opposite.

The contents of the bin will settle over time, so you may never actually fill it to the top. After 6 months or so, or when the bin is full, stop adding to it.

You now have 3 options:

1 Do nothing until the compost is ready to use. If you want to use the bin again immediately, remove it and cover the heap with a plastic sheet instead.

2 Remove the bin, or the front of it. Take off the top layers of materials that have not yet composted and set them aside. Remove the mature compost for use. Replace the top layers in the bin, having adjusted the moisture levels (by watering or adding dry materials) if necessary and continue composting.

3 If there is little finished compost as yet, simply mix everything together, adjust the mixture as necessary, and replace it in the bin. You can then continue to add to the bin again, or leave it to mature.

When is it ready? See page 58.

Cool compost
plus points

- Works with smaller quantities of compost materials
- Little work involved

Cool compost
minus points

- Can take 12 months to produce compost
- Will not kill all weed seeds and diseases

A slow, cool heap is an effective method of composting that everyone can use – making compost in around 6-12 months. Be sure to balance your 'greens' and browns'.

Quick, hot composting

'Quick' composting can make compost in as little as 12 weeks
- if you have sufficient material, time and energy.

Stage 1 Build the heap

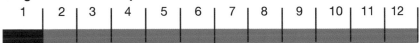

1 Gather enough mixed compostable materials to fill a good sized
compost bin all at once. Remember to balance 'greens' and 'browns'.

2 Chop tough and chunky items using a sharp spade or a shredder,
or simply bash them with a hammer to start the decomposition.

3 Soak very dry ingredients in water, or water them well.

4 Mix all the ingredients together, making sure that drier and tough items
are mixed with soft, wet materials.

5 Fill the compost bin. Firm the contents down gently, particularly around
the edges, every metre or so. Water anything that still looks dry.

6 Cover the bin.

Stage 2 – The bugs get going

1 Within a few days the middle of the heap should be hot; it may even be steaming in cold weather. This heat shows that the microbes are working overtime, chomping their way through the soft 'greens'. The heat speeds up the composting process, and also helps to kill weed seeds and disease organisms.

2 After a week or two the heap will cool as the microbes run out of air and stop working. Encourage a second heating by taking everything out of the bin, fluffing it up, watering dry areas then putting it back. This is known as turning the heap.

3 You may like to turn the heap a second time.

'Quick' composting can make compost in as little as 12 weeks – if you have sufficient material, time and energy.

Stage 3 – Larger creatures move in

1 The rate of activity in a heap slows as the composters move on to the tougher ingredients - so an older heap does not heat up. Worms, beetles and other creatures, that prefer cooler conditions, will move in.

2 Leave the heap to mature.

Stage 4 – Use the compost

Quick compost **plus points:**

- 12 week turnaround

- Kills many disease organisms

- Kills many weed seeds

Quick composting: After a week or two the heap will cool as the microbes run out of air and stop working. Encourage a second heating by taking everything out of the bin, fluffing it up, watering dry areas then putting it back. This is known as turning the heap. You may like to turn the heap a second time.

Compost **trouble shooting**

Problem

Compost heap smells unpleasant, contents soggy and slimy.

Causes and solutions

This usually happens when the proportion of 'greens' is too high. Check bin drainage and improve if necessary. Mix in drier materials such as crumpled paper and card, old plants etc. to balance the 'greens'.

Problem

Clouds of tiny black flies appear when the lid of the bin is removed.

Causes and solutions

These are fruit flies, and they are totally harmless. They are most common in summer, where there is a lot of kitchen waste in a heap. Empty your kitchen waste collection bucket daily, and bury its contents in the heap, or cover it well with other ingredients. Leave the compost bin lid ajar to allow the flies to come and go, so they don't build up into clouds.

Problem

No compost. The contents of the bin remain relatively unchanged for months.

Causes and solutions

The ingredients of the heap are too tough and dry for the compost process to start. Empty the compost bin. Chop or shred tough items. Mix with wetter, softer ingredients. Water if necessary. Refill the compost bin.

Problem

Tiny white flies and various other creepy crawlies, including some slugs, are visible in the compost bin.

Causes and solutions

These creatures are simply part of the mixed population that is involved in the composting process. Do nothing. A compost heap does not breed pests and diseases that will attack garden plants. Never apply a pesticide to a compost heap - you will kill the very creatures that make the compost.

Problem

The compost looks ready to use but there are eggshells, sweet corn cobs and bits of stick still visible.

Causes and solutions

These items are very slow to decay, so do stay around in a recognisable form for longer than most. The compost is perfectly safe to use in this state.

Problem

Weed seedlings appear from compost that has been spread on the garden.

Causes and solutions

Weed seeds may have been added to the compost heap with the weeds; they may have been blown in if the heap has been left uncovered. A hot heap will kill many weed seeds, but slower methods will not. Hoe the weeds off when young - or dig the compost into the ground rather than spreading it as a mulch. To reduce the incidence of weed seeds in the compost, weed the garden regularly so weed plants do not have time to set seed. Also keep the heap covered.

If possible, make a hot heap.

Weed seedlings will sometimes appear in compost spread on the soil. Simply hoe weeds off regularly.

action stations

1 **Get started!**

2 **Use the cool heap method** if you haven't got much material to compost.

3 **Go for the hot heap** if you've lots to compost at once.

4 **Don't worry too much about it.** The compost creatures do most of the work.

5

The fun bit!

Using your compost in the garden

Use compost (and leafmould) regularly and you will see your garden bloom. If your garden is already thriving, then compost will keep it that way. If it is struggling, the effects of feeding it with compost will be more obvious. Plants – and this includes grass – will generally look healthier and stay in good condition for longer in the season. Your vegetables will give better crops, over a longer period, and need less watering. Research is now proving that plants grown in composted soil are less prone to pest and disease attack and therefore do not require the use of chemical pesticides. Something that compost users have always known!

Compost can be used as soon as it has gone dark in colour, and you can no longer recognise the original ingredients, apart from eggshells, twigs and corn cobs which are very resistant to decay. It may be fine and crumbly, or it may be lumpy, slimy or sticky. Whatever the quality, you can use it on the garden.

The perfect preparation for a season of blooms.

53

Black 'gold' – use it where it's needed most.

Using compost

- Use it anywhere in the garden to improve the soil and feed the plants.

- If quantities are limited, use it on plants that need a rich soil that doesn't dry out quickly.

- Apply in the spring or summer, to growing plants, or to a site that is to be planted up.

- Use it at a rate of up to 1 large wheelbarrow full per 5 square metres.

- Spread it as a surface mulch or dig it in to the top few inches of soil where plant roots feed. Don't bury it deep.

- If the compost tends to grow lots of weed seedlings, hoe these off.

- Add an inch or two to pots and planters in the spring.

- Use as an ingredient in home-made potting mixes.

Where the soil is already in reasonable condition, do not apply compost to annual flowers (it will encourage leafy growth rather than blooms) or to herbs and shrubs, such as rosemary and other Mediterranean type plants, that prefer a poor, well drained soil.

Vegetables

Apply before sowing/planting or spread as a mulch on the soil around growing plants

Potatoes	*Courgettes*	*Cucumbers*
Leeks	*Pumpkins*	*Spinach*
Chard	*Cabbage family*	*Tomatoes*

Herbs

Apply to soil before sowing/planting or spread as a mulch on the soil around growing plants

Parsley	*Mint*	*Chives*	*Coriander*

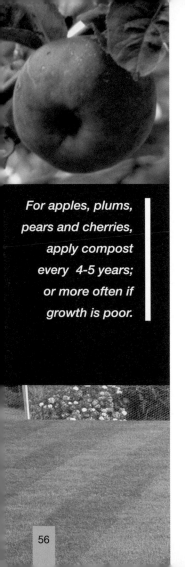

For apples, plums, pears and cherries, apply compost every 4-5 years; or more often if growth is poor.

Ornamentals and **fruit**

Apply compost before planting. Spread as a mulch on the soil around existing plants. Cover an area of ground of about 1sq m around each tree or bush.

Roses and other shrubs that are pruned hard regularly – apply compost every 2 years.

Herbaceous perennials (those that die down and come up again each year) – apply compost every 2 or 3 years.

Apples, plums, pears, cherries – apply compost every 4-5 years; more often if growth is poor.

Blackcurrants, raspberries – apply compost every 3 years.

Gooseberries – apply compost every 4-5 years.

Lawns

Use fine or sieved compost.

Spread over surface of the lawn in spring or summer every few years, or more often if growth is poor.

Use **worms to turbo-charge** your composting!

Although many of us are squeamish about worms, they are very useful. They're clean, efficient and the fastest natural composters by a mile – they can eat half their own body weight in waste every single day!

Worms will move into a garden compost heap naturally in the final stages of the composting process. You can also set up a 'stand alone' worm composting system, which is a really good way of recycling kitchen scraps all year round. Unlike the standard method of composting, a worm system thrives on a regular input of small quantities of waste.

How do I do it?

Most people buy what is called a 'wormery' or you can convert a plastic dustbin (see the Resources section on page 63 for suppliers). Wormeries are specially designed bins to make it easy, with instructions and a pouring tap to take the liquid feed off. They also come with a pack of the right kind of hungry worms to get you off to a good start. Why put your kitchen waste into landfill when you can feed it to the worms and get back 'black gold' for your garden?

Your composting **questions answered**

Is garden compost the same as the 'multipurpose' and potting composts that are sold in garden centres?

No. 'Multipurpose' and potting composts are mixes designed specifically for raising and growing plants in pots. Garden compost can be used as an ingredient of a home-made potting compost, but is not suitable on its own.

Can I buy the equivalent of garden compost?

Yes. The most commonly available is green waste compost – the product of large scale composting plants. Because it is made primarily from prunings and other tougher waste it is not such a rich mix as garden compost – but will improve the soil. Various types of composted animal manures and vegetable wastes are also available.

When is compost ready to use?

Compost is ready to use when it is a dark brown colour and the original ingredients cannot be recognised - apart from the odd eggshell or twig.

It may be sweet smelling and crumbly or it may be a bit sticky, stringy, slimy or lumpy; all will be quite useable.

Is it safe to make and use compost with children around?

Yes – as long as the usual hygiene precautions of washing hands etc are kept to. Never include used cat litter, or dog faeces in the heap, and if it contains other animal manures, make sure it is well composted before use.

Can I compost poisonous plants or will they poison the soil and my vegetables?

Poisonous plants can be composted quite safely. The poisons will be broken down in the composting process.

Can I compost diseased plants?

Don't compost plants with diseases such as white rot, sclerotinia, wilts and clubroot that can persist in the soil. Many diseases only survive on living plants – so will not survive in a compost heap.

How long does it take to make compost?

Anything from 12 weeks to a year or so, depending on the method you use. Leafmould can take 1-2 years.

Comfrey is a good compost 'activator', rich in easily accessible nitrogen.

Do I need special equipment to make compost?

No. All you really need is a compost bin. You may find that your local authority will supply a bin at a low price.

Is it safe to compost colour printed paper and cardboard?

Yes. The inks used nowadays do not contain heavy metal.

Is it safe to put laurel prunings through a shredder?

Careful! When shredding laurel and other poisonous shrubs, always work outside. **Wear a dust mask and gloves.**

action stations

1 **Apply compost and leafmould** as a surface mulch which helps retain moisture and keep weeds down, or dig it in to the top few inches of soil as a compost.

2 **Apply compost in the spring and summer.**

3 **Where compost supplies are limited,** use it on plants that prefer a rich soil.

4 **Leafmould** can be used anywhere at any time of year.

Want more organic gardening help?

Then join HDRA, the national charity
for organic gardening, farming and food.

As a member of HDRA you'll gain-

- free access to our Gardening Advisory Service
- access to our three gardens in Warwickshire, Kent and Essex and to 10 more gardens around the UK
- opportunities to attend courses and talks or visit other gardens on Organic Gardens Open Weekends
- discounts when ordering from the Organic Gardening Catalogue
- discounted membership of the Heritage Seed Library
- quarterly magazines full of useful information

You'll also be supporting-

- the conservation of heritage seeds
- an overseas organic advisory service to help small-scale farmers in the tropics
- Duchy Originals HDRA Organic Gardens for Schools
- HDRA Organic Food For All campaign
- research into organic agriculture

To join HDRA ring: **024 7630 3517**
email: **enquiries@hdra.org.uk**
or visit our website: **www.hdra.org.uk**

Charity No. 298104

▌Resources

HDRA the organic organisation
promoting organic gardening
farming and food
www.hdra.org.uk
024 7630 3517

Soil Association the heart of
organic food and farming
www.soilassociation.org
0117 929 0661

The Composting Association
www.compost.org.uk
0870160 3270

WRAP
Home composting helpline
0845 600 0323

Composting displays to visit
Ryton Organic Gardens,
Coventry CV8 3LG 024 7630 3517
www.hdra.org.uk/gardens/ryton.htm

Yalding Organic Gardens
Benover Road, Yalding, Maidstone,
Kent ME18 6EX 01622 814650

Books
The HDRA Encyclopedia of
Organic Gardening
Dorling Kindersley
editor Pauline Pears

Local Authorities
Many local authorities provide
advice on home composting

MAIL ORDER:

The Organic Gardening Catalogue
Organic seeds, composts, raised
beds, barriers, traps and other
organic gardening sundries. All
purchases help to fund the HDRA's
charity work.
www.organiccatalogue.com
0845 1301304

Centre for Alternative Technology
www.cat.org.uk 01654 705950

Green Gardener
www.greengardener.co.uk
01394 420087

Wiggly Wigglers
www.wigglywigglers.co.uk
0800 216990

who, what, where, when and why organic?

for all the answers and tempting offers go to www.whyorganic.org

- Mouthwatering offers on organic produce
- Organic places to shop and stay across the UK
- Seasonal recipes from celebrity chefs
- Expert advice on your food and health
- Soil Association food club – join for just £1 a month

Soil Association
the heart of organic food & farming